When you begin to use this book,
please check here:

If you find this book lying about
and the above box is checked,
<u>please</u> don't read any further.
This is someone's private, confidential notebook.
Please respect his or her privacy.

Thank you.

*This space
will be used for
quotes and poems.*

This is *your* book of surviving, healing and growing.
If there's anything in this book
you don't want to do,

DON'T DO IT!

In fact, only do the things you really *want* to do.
(We didn't like the "have to" stuff in school, either.)

If we ask you to write something
and you want to draw a picture, great.

If we ask you to draw a picture
and you want to write a poem, write the poem.

Follow your heart.

This book is designed to be used along with the revised and expanded edition of *How to Survive the Loss of a Love.* That book has ninety-four main suggestions for surviving, healing and growing. This workbook contains ninety-four exercises—one per numbered suggestion in *How to Survive the Loss of a Love.*

Before doing each numbered exercise in this book, we recommend you read the correspondingly numbered main suggestion in *How to Survive the Loss of a Love.* (That is, before doing exercise "Three" in this book, read suggestion "Three" in *How to Survive the Loss of a Love.*)

As each suggestion in *How to Survive the Loss of a Love* is a page (or less) in length, this only takes a few minutes.

Reading the text in *How to Survive the Loss of a Love* first is not absolutely necessary. (This workbook is complete in itself.) We do, however, highly recommend it.

If there's a name under the quote or poem— that's who wrote it.

If you have a copy of *How to Survive the Loss of a Love* prior to the revised edition (the revised edition was published in 1991), the numbers will not match up. (For the revised edition, we added thirty-six new suggestions.) Most of the *headings*, however, remain the same. A little flipping through an old edition will reveal many of the points covered by exercises in this book.

(We do, of course, encourage you to get the new edition. There's new information in it we consider valuable—that's why we revised the earlier edition!)

If you don't have a copy of *How to Survive the Loss of a Love* on hand (in any edition), please do not wait to start this book. Pick up a copy of *How to Survive the Loss of a Love* when you have a chance.

Meanwhile, turn the page and begin now.

If there's no name under the poem, it was written by our own Peter McWilliams.

How to Survive the Loss of a Love
is also available on unabridged audiocassettes,
read by the authors.

❦

The newly revised edition of
How to Survive the Loss of a Love
is available in hardcover.

❦

All poetry not attributed to a specific author is from
Come Love with Me & Be My Life:
The Collected Romantic Poetry of Peter McWilliams.

All available at your local bookstore
or by calling

1-800-LIFE-101

or you can write to

Prelude Press
8165 Mannix Drive
Los Angeles, CA 90046

THANK YOU!

Surviving, Healing & Growing

by

Melba Colgrove, Ph.D.,
Harold Bloomfield, M.D.,
& Peter McWilliams

Published by
Prelude Press
8165 Mannix Drive
Los Angeles, California 90046

Cover Design: Paul LeBus
Desktop Publishing: Sara J. Thomas

Published simultaneously in the United States and Canada
Distributed by Bantam Books

One: *You Will Survive*

Say aloud, "I am alive. I will survive."
Repeat aloud ten times as you write it here:

I am alive.
I will survive.

....

....

....

....

....

....

....

It is the truth.
You *are* alive.
You *will* survive.

What are some of the losses you have survived?

_____

_____

_____

_____

_____

_____

_____

_____

_____

_____

_____

_____

Bridges built to the sun,

they burn don't they ?

11

If you *were* to need help, what would you do? Whom would you call? Where would you go?

Pretend you are doing research for a friend. Please do the following:

Call directory assistance and ask for the number of the local Suicide Prevention Hotline. Write the number here:

_____

Look in the Yellow Pages under Help Lines. If there's no listing under Help Lines, call directory assistance and ask what other heading they might suggest. Write down at least two of the numbers here:

_____

_____

Do you know any health professionals (psychologists, psychiatrists, counselors, etc.)? If so, write the name and number of at least two of them here:

_____

_____

If friends have offered to help, call and ask each of them, "Would it be all right if I called you anytime, 24 hours a day?" Write the names and numbers of friends who say yes here:

_____

_____

Although you may never need them, it's good to know you can turn directly to this page and dial any of the above numbers any time of the day or night.

Three: *Acknowledge the Loss*

*Separating
the memory
of yesterday's warmth
from
the reality
of today's rejection
is a difficult
painful
tedious
exacting
but highly
necessary task.*

*You simply no longer
love me.
You simply never will.*

How complex.

What is the loss (or losses) you are currently experiencing? That is, what have you lost?

....

....

....

....

....

....

....

What "smaller" or not-so-obvious losses have you suffered as a result or since?

....

....

....

....

....

....

....

List ten people you know personally who have survived a loss. What did they lose?

_____

_____

_____

_____

_____

_____

_____

_____

_____

_____

At first you thought I was The Perfect Human Being.

I should have known that in your eyes the only way I could go was down hill.

List ten celebrities (or other fictional characters) who have suffered a loss.

Scarlett O'Hara, Tara, Rhett, Melanie, Bonnie, The South,

Ashley, Charles Hamilton, Aunt Pittypat,

Saying
good night
you
leave,
sentencing
me to a
bad
one.

15

Circle or highlight the ones you're feeling now:

SILLY

loathful

indecisive

Shock

Numb

Relieved

grief-stricken

Angry

inferior

Frightened

FEAR

Envious

melancholy

lost

happy

LIKE A FAILURE

suicidal

full of self-hatred

giddy

Exhausted

Good

Pain

overwhelmed

muddled

beaten

OUTRAGED

disgusted

16

*Pain
is
discovering
there
is
nothing
left
to
discover.*

Sit down, close your eyes
(after reading this page, of course),
and feel whatever feelings or sensations
are in your body.

Whatever you feel
(numbness, fear, anger, pain),
accept it.

Let it be OK.

Whatever is, is.

Do this for two minutes.
(Longer, if you wish.)

Six: *Be with the Pain*

Draw a simple outline of your body.
Where in your body do you feel pain?
Circle that area.

Draw a picture of what your pain looks and feels like.

If possible, use crayons or colored pens.
You might want to use your nondominant hand
(if right-handed, use your left, and vice versa).

Look at the drawing of your pain on the previous page.

What emotions are you feeling?

Did you leave anything out? If so, feel free to add it now.

Add some words or sounds to the drawing. Examples might include,

"Ow" "Moan" "Help"

"Why won't you love me?"

"Why did you desert me?"

"How can they do this to me?"

"Have you forgotten me?" "I'm numb"

"Go away" "Sick" "Tired"

"I want you back" "Weak"

Who will say
the final
good bye
first,
and who will
make it last:

me and my pain,
or
you and your fear?

Describe your pain:

....

....

....

....

....

....

....

....

....

....

....

....

....

....

*I am over-run,
jungled in my bed,
I am infested with a
menagerie of desires;
my heart is eaten
by a dove,
hounds in my head
obey a whipmaster
who cries nothing but
havoc as the hours
test my endurance
with an accumula-
tion of tortures.*

ELIZABETH SMART

Seven: *You're Great!*

Enthusiastic	Adventuresome
Courageous	Foolhardy
Vulnerable	Brave
Alive	Breathing
Carefree	Careful
Considerate	Kind
Giving	Loving
Receiving	Understanding
Appreciative	Caring
Funny	Romantic
Intuitive	Reliable
Receptive	Emotional
Committed	Determined
Uncommitted	Free
Unconditional	Neutral
Patient	Devoted
Tender	Warm
Colorful	Valuing
Dedicated	Spiritual
Religious	Grateful
Joyful	

Circle those qualities that apply to you (even occasionally).

Circle those qualities your friends would say apply to you.

Add to the list the fact that you're committed to your own surviving, healing and growing by working in this book.

Add any other qualities we forgot.

Eight: *Give Yourself Time to Heal*

Write 10 to 20 times: "I am alive. I will survive."

I hope I heal soon.

I want to enjoy Autumn.

Nine: *The Healing Process Has Its Progressions and Regressions*

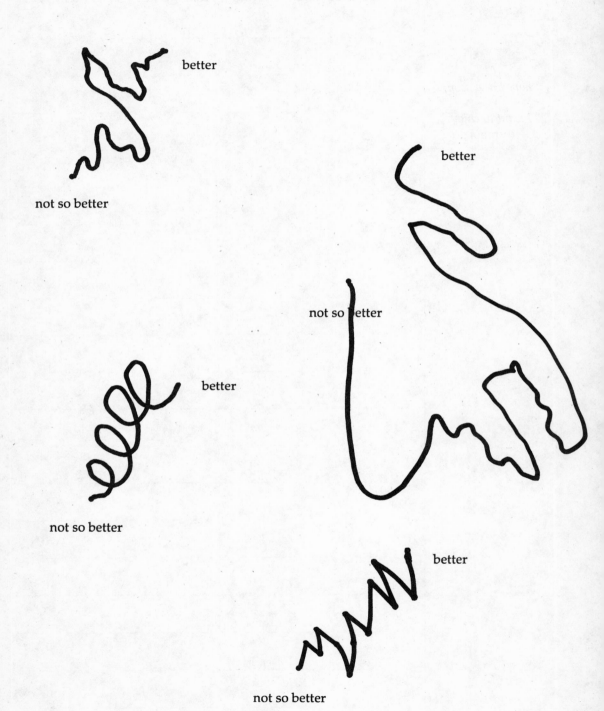

better

not so better

better

not so better

better

not so better

better

not so better

Now draw the graph of your own survival.
(However it goes, be sure to end up at "better.")

• better

•

not so better

How many "tomorrows" have successfully come for you? (Multiply 365 times your age.)

365 X _____ = _____

Congratulations!

I was not ready for you,
but you seemed quite
ready for me.

trapped in a week.
drained in a month.
deserted in forty days.

Forty days. deserted.

Jesus spent forty days
in a desert once.
He was tempted by
the devil.
We are told he resisted
temptation.

fortunately
for The Pope
The Archbishop
of Canterbury
and Billy Graham
you were not the devil.

Christianity might
never have
gotten off the ground.

Eleven: *Breathe!*

Take a slow, deep breath (all the way down to your lower abdomen).

Exhale fully.

Take another slow, deep breath.

Feel what you feel.

Breathe again.

Breathe in the positive.

Breathe out the negative.

Breathe in compassion. Breathe out harshness.

Breathe in forgiveness. Breathe out judgements.

Breathe in love. Breathe out hatred.

Breathe in light. Breathe out darkness.

I don't know whether I'm being tested or forgotten.

Twelve: *Get Lots of Rest—Now*

Spend at least one hour doing one or more of the following:

- Take a nap.

- Meditate.

- Contemplate.

- Pray.

- Spend time quietly in nature (walk on a beach, stroll through a park, talk to your plants, pet your pets, or watch a nature video).

- Take a hot bath.

- Soak your feet.

- Listen to restful music.

- Think quietly, "Peace. Be still."

- Go to bed.

I was overcome, and now undone.

this September will be happily remembered

as soon as it can be fully forgotten.

Make a list of things you can do in bed:

....

....

....

....

....

....

....

....

....

....

....

....

....

Leave me here.
Go away.
Love
will come
another
day.

I will rain
until one
takes my
hand
and offers
sun.

What are five things
you must do today, no matter what?
(HINTS: Breathe, eat something, take a bath,
make a phone call, get dressed.)

....

....

....

....

....

....

....

....

I must give you up.
I must give you up.
I must give you up.
I must give you up.
I must give you up.
I must give you up.
I must give you up.
I must give you up.
I must give you up.
I must give you up.
I must give you up.
I must give you up.
I must give you up.
I must give you up.
I must give you up.
I must give you up.
I must give you up.
I must survive.
I must give you up.
I must give you up.
I must give you up.
I must give you up.
I must give you up.
I must give you up.

Now, do at least one of them.

Fourteen: *Keep Decision-Making to a Minimum*

List six things you're *not* going
to decide about for at least a month:
(HINTS: Moving, changing jobs, major buying or
selling, quitting smoking, losing weight, finding a new
romance.)

_____

_____

_____

_____

_____

The date one month from today is

_____

If you worry about any of the things on
the list before the above date, tell yourself, "I'll decide about that after
_____."

(date above)

I want to go back.

*Back to the time
when your feelings
for me were so
strong that I was
afraid.*

*Back to a time
when I received
poems in the mail
and I could call you
and hear a smile.*

*Back to a time
when we made plans
that, at the time,
were realistic.*

Fifteen: *It's OK to Make "Silly" Misteaks*

Circle any of these common silly mistakes you have accomplished:

- Lock your keys in your car.

- Lock your keys in another person's car.

- Lock another person's keys in your car.

- Lock yourself out of the house.

- Forget your best friend's name.

- Misspell your own name.

- Misspell anything three times in a row.

- Overdraw your bank account.

- Overeat.

- Forget an appointment.

- Forget your wallet or purse.

- Forget if you have a wallet or a purse.

- Forget anything.

- Burn dinner.

- Forget to make dinner.

- Forget to turn on the oven.

- Look for glasses you're wearing.

When pain strikes,
we often ask
the wrong questions,
such as, Why me?
The right questions are,
What can I
learn from this?
What can I do
about it?
What can I accomplish
in spite of it?

NORMAN VINCENT
PEALE

What "silly" mistakes have you made?

Find a picture or drawing from a newspaper or magazine to
illustrate one of your mistakes.

Cut it out and paste it here, or draw your own.

Sixteen: *It's OK to Go through the Motions in Slow Motion*

Imagine a mouthful of peanut butter.
What would talking sound like?
Talk that way.

Imagine you have
a ten-pound weight in each hand.
Imagine lifting your arms over your head.
How much struggle would that take?
Pantomime that struggle.

Imagine yourself waist-deep in warm Jello.
What would it be like to walk in that?
How fast (or slow) would you be able to walk?
Now, get up and walk that way.

Imagine you have a ball and chain
shackled to your ankles.
What would walking be like?
Imitate that walk.

Wash your hands in slow motion
(take at least four minutes).

*It does not matter how
slowly you go so long
as you do not stop.*

CONFUCIUS

In what other ways have you been going through the motions in slow motion?

....

....

....

....

....

....

....

....

....

....

....

....

....

....

*Sorrow you can hold,
however desolating,
if nobody
speaks to you.
If they speak to you,
you break down.*

BEDE JARRETT

Seventeen: *It's OK to Need Comforting*

What comforts you? (*Not* the person or thing you lost.)

....

....

....

What comforted you as a child?

....

....

....

Do at least *one* of the above, or any one from the list below:

- Cuddle with a teddy bear.
- Get a massage.
- Buy (or make) yourself a treat.
- Lie in the sun.
- Do something with a friend.
- Watch your favorite movie.
- Visit a museum.
- Read your favorite magazine.
- Buy yourself flowers.
- Drink warm low-fat milk (or herbal tea).
- Exercise.
- Don't exercise.
- Have a good cry.
- Get a hug.
- Give a hug.

Eighteen: *Seek the Support of Others*

*When there are
joys
I want you for
sharing.*

*When there are
sorrows
I want you for
comfort.*

*I guess I'm leaning
on your memory
a little too much.*

Who are the people you can count on?
(Examples: Clergy, counselors, friends, family doctor,
coworkers, members of organizations, family.)

....

....

....

....

....

....

....

....

....

....

....

....

Call three of these people.

Make a plan to get together with at least
one of them.

Nineteen: *Touching and Hugging*

Do at least one of the following:

Put your hands over your heart.
Feel the healing energy
flowing from your hands into your heart.
Can you feel your heart beating?
Take a few minutes to feel yourself heal your-
self.

Put your hands on at least two other parts
of your body that feel numb,
hurting or in need of touching.

Rub your skin briskly with your hands,
a dry towel, body brush or luffa sponge.
This sheds dead skin and stimulates circulation.
Do this all over your body.

Anoint yourself with oil
(the bathtub is a good place to do this).
Rub oil (olive oil or a good massage oil)
on your body and gently massage yourself.
Now get some romaine lettuce and,
oh, never mind.

Take a hot bath.
Slowly soap and massage yourself.

Massage your feet, thoroughly and deeply.

Why had I waited so long, making excuses to myself that I needed the perfect moment? There is no such thing as the perfect moment. We make all our moments, and by the truth and love we bring to them, we make them perfect.

FRANCES
SHARKEY, M.D.

Ask a willing friend
—someone with whom you feel safe—
to hold you.
Ask your friend to sit on the floor
with his or her back against a wall (for support).
Then have him or her cradle you.
Or lie back in his or her arms.
Allow yourself to be embraced.
Take the time to relax into the nurturing.
Whatever you feel—from tears to joy—is OK.

Ask friends for hugs.
If no one's around, hug yourself.
Hugging a pet or a tree works well, too.
If you are spiritually inclined,
ask God to hug you.
Then try hugging God.

HUGS PER DAY:

3 for survival   5 for healing   8 for growth

Like a dance card, you can have a hug card.
Here's today's hug card:

*Take a look
at those two open
hands of yours.
They are tools with
which to serve,
make friends,
and reach out
for the best in life.
Open hands open the
way to achievement.
Put them to work
today.*

WILFRED A.
PETERSON

Hug Card	
1. *Myself*	5. *Myself*
2. _____	6. _____
3. *Myself*	7. *Myself*
4. *A tree*	8. _____

Twenty: *Find Others Who Have Survived a Similar Loss*

Get a Yellow Pages. Look under "Human Service Organizations." Read the listings under that heading. Do any of the groups sound as though they might be of assistance or support to you? If so, write them here:

....

....

....

....

....

....

....

....

....

Call one.

It is one of the mysteries of our nature that a man, all unprepared, can receive a thunderstroke like that and live. There is but one reasonable explanation of it. The intellect is stunned by the shock and but gropingly gathers the meaning of the words. The power to realize their full import is mercifully wanting.

MARK TWAIN
On receiving a telegram
of his daughter's death

Since the beginning of time, approximately how many people have suffered a loss such as yours? (Go ahead, take a guess.)

_____

Can you think of any historical or fictional characters who suffered a similar loss?

_____

_____

_____

_____

_____

_____

_____

Warm summer sun,
shine kindly here;
Warm southern wind,
blow softly here;
Green sod above,
lie light, lie light—
Good-night, dear heart,
good-night,
good-night.

MARK TWAIN
Epitaph for his daughter

41

Twenty-one: *Seek Wise Guidance*

Who are the wise people in your life?

....

....

....

....

....

....

....

....

....

*Friendship is the
finest balm for the
pangs of despised love.*

JANE AUSTEN

In some way, contact at least one of them.

What would you tell your closest friend in a situation just like yours? Contact the wisdom within yourself and use it to answer this question.

_____

_____

_____

_____

_____

_____

_____

_____

_____

_____

*All those who try
to go it sole alone,
Too proud to be be-
holden for relief,
Are absolutely sure
to come to grief.*

ROBERT FROST

Twenty-two: *Surround Yourself with Things That Are Alive*

Draw a picture of yourself surrounded by things that are alive—calming plants, nurturing animals, helpful humans. (By this definition, "alive" also includes the ocean, mountains or any other offspring of Mother Earth.)

(If you don't like to draw, go buy yourself a plant.)

Other suggestions:

- Go to the zoo.

- Adopt a pet.

- Walk through a park.

- Plant something.

- Visit someone with a new baby.

- Go to a live play, performance, concert or event.

The human spirit is stronger than anything that can happen to it.

C. C. SCOTT

Twenty-three: *Reaffirm Your Beliefs*

What is your belief/view/conception of God/Higher Power/Spirit/Supreme Being/Mother Nature?

....

....

....

....

....

We all live in the lap of infinite intelligence.

EMERSON

What book best represents that belief to you?

....

Open that book randomly and read at least one page from it now. Write your favorite passage from that page below:

....

....

....

....

....

They that sow in tears shall reap in joy. He that goeth forth and weepeth, bearing precious seed, shall doubtless come again with rejoicing, bringing his sheaves with him.

PSALMS
126:5-6

Twenty-four: *Sundays Are the Worst*

Arrange now to do something from your (or our) list of comforting things (page 36) this Sunday or upcoming holiday (whichever is coming first).

This weekend/holiday I will do these comforting activities:

....

....

....

....

....

....

....

....

There's not much left, and very little's right.

Twenty-five: *The Question of Suicide*

Thoughts of suicide during a recovery from loss are natural and common. If you feel you might *act* on such thoughts, seek help at once. (Call telephone information and ask for Suicide Hotline, go to your local hospital emergency room, or see a psychiatrist or mental health professional at once.)

Who (or what) would miss you (even a little) if you were no longer around?

_____

_____

_____

_____

_____

_____

_____

_____

Suicide is the extraordinary propensity of the human being to join hands with external forces in an attack on his own existence.

KARL MENNINGER

What would you miss (people, things, experiences, future events) if they were taken from your life?

....

....

....

....

....

....

....

....

....

....

(Suicide is the loss of all the above—and everything else!)
Say aloud ten times: "I may not enjoy every minute of it, but I am alive. I will survive."

What are you still curious about? (What are the books you haven't read? What are the movies you haven't seen—or want to see again? What are the "personal dramas" in your "real life" that have yet to reach a conclusion? Don't you wonder whether this planet will make it to the next millennium?

Suicide is a belated acquiescence in the opinion of one's wife's relatives.

H. L. MENCKEN

What do you still appreciate about life even though you're in loss?

_____

_____

_____

_____

_____

What will you be able to appreciate once you heal more fully?

_____

_____

_____

_____

_____

_____

Be glad of life because it gives you the chance to love and to work and to play and to look at the stars.

HENRY VAN DYKE

HEALING

It isn't for the moment you are
stuck that you need courage,
but for the long uphill climb back to
sanity and faith and security.

ANNE MORROW LINDBERG

Twenty-six: *Do Your Mourning Now*

Give yourself some crying time.

If you prefer crying alone, turn the phone off and put a "DO NOT DISTURB" sign on your door.

If you cry more easily with other people, the right person would feel privileged to support you.

You might also try one of these suggestions:

1. Look at mementos, photos, love letters, video tapes, home movies or any other reminders of who or what was lost.

2. Rent a movie or watch a TV show known to elicit tears—especially one that parallels your loss.

3. Play songs or music that evoke sadness.

Let yourself feel the grief.

To weep is to make less the depth of grief.

SHAKESPEARE

Complete these sentences:

I mourn because _____

_____

_____

I feel sad because _____

_____

_____

I can't accept _____

_____

_____

I cry about _____

_____

_____

I still care about _____

_____

_____

I wish _____

_____

_____

How could...have happened? _____

_____

I can't believe that _____

_____

_____

I grieve for _____

_____

_____

*Give sorrow words;
the grief
that does not speak
Whispers the o'er-
fraught heart and
bids it break.*

SHAKESPEARE

55

Draw a picture of what your sadness looks and feels like.

If possible, use crayons.
If you're right-handed,
you might want to use your left hand, and vice versa.

Give your sadness a voice. Ask it these questions, and listen to what it answers. Write down the answers.

Sadness, do I embarrass you by talking to you?

_____

_____

Sadness, where do you live in my body?

_____

_____

Sadness, what is it I can't accept?

_____

_____

Sadness, what must I do to heal more fully?

_____

_____

Sadness, what can I do right now to help me survive?

_____

_____

Sadness, what other information do you have for me?

_____

_____

For, although
it is true
that fear and despair
can overwhelm us,
hope cannot
be purchased with the
refusal to feel.

SUSAN GRIFFIN

Sadness, what gift do you have for me?

_____

_____

Thank the sadness for speaking with you. Put your hands on the place on your body where you feel the sadness. In your imagination, surround the sadness with a white light. Give your sadness a hug.

Twenty-seven: *Earlier Losses May Surface*

Have any previous losses come to mind during this loss? If so, what are they?

_____

_____

_____

_____

_____

_____

_____

_____

_____

_____

_____

*Tears, idle tears,
I know not
what they mean,
Tears from the depth of
some divine despair
Rise in the heart,
and gather to the eyes,
In looking on the
happy autumn fields,
And thinking of the
days that are no more.*

ALFRED,
LORD TENNYSON

Any losses from childhood?

_____

_____

_____

_____

_____

_____

What losses from adolescence and adult life still haunt you?

_____

_____

_____

_____

_____

_____

Once upon a time, and a very long time ago it was, too, I was innocent.

I did not know what love was.

Pain was when you fell from a tree.

If other losses have surfaced, they may be healing now. Let them heal fully.

Twenty-eight: *Be Gentle with Yourself*

Make a list of the things you say to yourself that are harsh or critical:

How could I be so stupid?

I'm no good.

Nobody loves me.

It's my fault.

Leave my life
quickly,

as quickly as you came.

Give me pain
and desolation
as quickly
and intensely as
you gave love and lust.

Don't let me
fall   a   part.

Go,
leaving a crumpled me
&
no forwarding address

List ways in which you
could be more gentle with yourself:

I forgive myself.

I am good.

I love myself.

Things happen.

*Come
over
and we will
over
come
that which has
come
over
us*

How has your healing gone thus far?
Draw a graph. Has it been full of ups and downs?
Plot that below:

● Today

The Loss ●

How have others expected you to heal?
(Is it more like a straight line—always "upward and onward"?)

● Today

The Loss ●

List the ten most impatient pieces of advice you have been given thus far in your loss:

1. *You're wallowing in this, aren't you?*

2. *He/she's not worth it!*

3. *You still haven't gotten over this?*

4. *You're just feeling sorry for yourself.*

It is hard to know what to say to a person who has been struck by tragedy, but it is easier to know what not to say. Anything critical of the mourner ("don't take it so hard," "try to hold back your tears, you're upsetting people") is wrong. Anything which tries to minimize the mourner's pain ("it's probably for the best," "it could be a lot worse," "she's better off now") is likely to be misguided and unappreciated. Anything which asks the mourner to disguise or reject his feelings ("we have no right to question God," "God must love you to have selected you for this burden") is wrong as well.

HAROLD S. KUSHNER

List ten statements of permission to heal at your own pace:

1. *I'm exactly where I need to be.*

2. *I'm worthy of healing fully.*

3. *I'll be over this when I'm over this.*

4. *I have every right to feel whatever I feel.*

Now *you* can look back on your healing process thus far and ask *yourself* (not others) what is left to do. Is there anything in the healing process thus far you've denied, covered up or pretended was "all better"?

If so, what is it?

_____

_____

_____

Why did you deny it?

_____

_____

_____

Can you face it now?

_____

_____

_____

What still needs to be healed?

_____

_____

_____

*Pain has an element
of blank;
It cannot recollect
When it began,
or if there were
A day
when it was not.
It has no future
but itself,
Its infinite realms
contain
Its past, enlightened
to perceive
New periods of pain.*

EMILY DICKINSON

Now would be a good time to repeat some exercises you've done, or perhaps to do some of the exercises you passed over.

Want a real challenge?
Do the one you wanted to do least.

Thirty: *Don't Try to Rekindle the Old Relationship*

On the next page, write a FINAL good-bye letter to the person or thing you lost. Say whatever you'd like him, her or it to know. (You will not be sending the letter, so be bold.) Then say good-bye, send your love, date it and sign it.

*You cannot come into
my life
again.*

*don't try to enter
my mind with
your eyes.*

it won't work.

*I am impenetrable.
aloof.
friendly, but distant.
kind, but cold.*

*this time
you haven't a chance.*

*and yet,
your ten minute visit
will cause
ten days
of pain.*

*how hard
the forgetting.
how easy
the remembering.
how cruel the process
that possesses me.*

Tear this page out of the book and burn it.*

*To love
is to be
vulnerable.*

*to love
you anymore
is to be
dumb.*

*Do this safely, of course. Over the toilet is nice. After dropping the ashes in the bowl, you can flush them from your life forever. While doing this you can say, over and over, "I release you and I am free."

Thirty-one: *Make a Pact with a Friend*

Call a friend and make an agreement.
Ask if he or she will agree to the contract below:

Contract

I, _____ agree to con-
tact (not just <u>try</u> to contact, but actually contact) my
friend _____ before attempting to
contact _____.

Dated: _____

Signed: _____

_____

Penalty for forfeiture: several nights of misery.

Thirty-two: *Mementos*

Time to clean house.

Go around collecting things
that remind you of the dead past.
Sell or donate the ones that are valuable
(starting with the engagement ring—
no engagement ring? That bastard!).
Discard the ones that aren't.

Take the time to mourn the loss of each item
if you feel an attachment to it—then let it go.

Treasures for the family album
(or your biographer) can be saved,
but, for now, hide them.
Put them into storage.
Get them out of sight.

*Dear Madam,
I have been shown in
the files of the War
Department a
statement of the
Adjutant-General of
Massachusetts that
you are the mother of
five sons who have
died gloriously on the
field of battle. I feel
how weak and fruitless
must be any words of
mine which should at-
tempt to beguile you
from the grief of a loss
so overwhelming.*

ABRAHAM LINCOLN
Letter to Mrs. Bixby
[November 21, 1864]

Draw a picture or make a collage of your joyful life
after fully growing through your loss.
(HINT: Use bright colors.)

Cut this page out and hang the other side of it
where you see it often.

Imagine it is a year from today. How will you look back on this experience? Write words of inspiration and comfort to yourself:

73

Thirty-four: *Expect to Feel Afraid*

What are the questions you fear?
What goes bump in your night?

Am I loveable?

Am I sexually inadequate?

Will I ever feel normal again?

Am I going insane?

How could God let this happen?

Will I ever be loved again?

Will I ever love again?

I have borne thirteen children and seen them most all sold off into slavery, and when I cried out with a mother's grief, none but Jesus heard.

SOJOURNER TRUTH
1851

What is your list of fears?

I fear _____

_____

_____

_____

_____

I am afraid that _____

_____

_____

_____

I am terrified of _____

_____

_____

_____

I feel scared about _____

_____

_____

_____

*Is there no pity
sitting in the clouds,
That sees into the
bottom of my grief?*

SHAKESPEARE

Add your fears to this page.

Fear of…Commitment

DARKNESS

Rejection

pain

WINNING

success

Loneliness

Abandonment

Looking foolish

Losing

People

RISKING

failure

unknown

suffering

76

What if...

What if I'm left alone?

What if I look foolish?

What if others disapprove of me?

What if I risk and fail?

What are the "What if's..." you fear?

_____

_____

_____

_____

_____

_____

_____

_____

_____

Add "So" to each of the sentences
on the previous page.

So what if I'm left alone?

So what if I look foolish?

So what if others disapprove of me?

So what if I risk and fail?

So whatever...I will survive, heal and grow.

*Do the thing you fear
and the death of fear
is certain.*

EMERSON

Draw a picture of what your fear looks and feels like.

Are you feeling depressed?
It *is* a part of loss.

Check which of these common symptoms
of depression apply to you now:

☐ Exploding in anger over small matters

☐ Regret

☐ Feeling left out or overlooked

☐ Feeling unappreciated
   or taken for granted

☐ Suffering head, neck, back,
   stomach or other physical aches
   with no physical disorder

☐ Lacking confidence

☐ Overeating or loss of appetite

☐ Withdrawing or isolating

☐ Difficulty in concentrating or remembering

☐ Change in sexual desire or functioning

☐ Rigidity or compulsiveness

☐ Worrying and despair

☐ Pessimism

l
lo
lov
love
love
love
Love
LOve
LOVe
LOVE
LOVE
LOVE
LOVe
pain
LOVe
LOVe
LOVe
LOve
pain
LOve
LOve
paiN
Love
love
paIN
love
love
love
pAIN
love
love
PAIN
love
PAIN
PAIN
love
PAIN
love
PAIN
PaIN
In
I
i

☐ Irritability and anger

☐ Restlessness

☐ Lack of motivation

☐ Fatigue and low energy

☐ Slowed speech, movement or reflexes

☐ Making many errors

☐ Indifference

☐ Lacking meaning and purpose

If you can't find at least five of these that apply to you, either you are (A) in denial, or (B) reading the wrong book. Each of these is an indicator that YOU ARE HEALING.

*Grief fills the room
up of my absent child,
Lies in his bed,
walks up and down
with me,
Puts on
his pretty looks,
repeats his words,
Remembers me of all
his gracious parts,
Stuffs out
his vacant garments
with his form.*

SHAKESPEARE

Thirty-six: *It's OK to Feel Anger*

Answer the questions on the following pages spontaneously, emotionally, "from the gut." Don't worry about grammar, style or correctness.

After writing the answers to these questions, do not reread them. Turn the page and keep writing.

You like it that I write poems about you.

Your ego takes some perverse pleasure in them.

You will cause enough pain to fill a book, and then send autographed copies to your friends.

What do you resent
about being in a loss situation?

_____

_____

_____

_____

_____

What do you resent
about the person or thing you lost?

_____

_____

_____

_____

_____

How long will you
stay this time,
I ask

An unfair question,
you respond.

An unfair answer,
I reply

I'm furious about _____

_____

_____

_____

I hate it when _____

_____

_____

_____

I want to yell or scream _____

_____

_____

_____

*Do you want love,
or do you just want
someone to drive the
loneliness
from your life?*

*Do you want me,
or would anyone do?*

*Do you want to
love in return,
or just respond?*

*I was not put upon this
earth to test your
reflexes.*

84

I'm disgusted by _____

_____

_____

_____

_____

I'm fed up with _____

_____

_____

_____

_____

I can't stand _____

_____

_____

_____

_____

It's dangerous to leave a lonely man alone.

You don't know what lies he'll tell about you.

Or worse,

what truths.

What's your revenge fantasy? You've been hurt. A part of you
wants to strike back. This is natural.*

Draw a picture of your rage
or a picture of your revenge fantasy.

*(Our lawyer insists that we advise you not to act upon these fantasies.
Violent thoughts and feelings are OK, violent behavior is not. If you feel
you may take vengeful action, see a health practitioner instead.)

Now tear pages 83-86 from the book and burn them.*

*To paraphrase
an ancient
Chinese Curse:

*May you love an
interesting
person.*

*Do this safely, of course. Over the toilet is nice. After dropping the ashes in the bowl, you can flush them from your life forever. While doing this you can say, over and over, "I release you and I am free."

To further release anger (if any)
try one or more of these "exorcises":

Beat a pillow.

Beat a couch.

Scream (a car with the windows closed
makes a good scream chamber).

Play piano at full crescendo.

I can throw a fit,
I'm a master at it.

MADONNA

Play "aggressive" tennis, handball, racquetball, or any other ball.

Hit a punching bag.

"Violently" knead bread.

"Furiously" clean house.
(Vacuuming and screaming go together nicely—it's also a good metaphor for "getting it out" and "cleaning it up.")

Do any of the above until you feel spent.

It takes courage to live—courage and strength and hope and humor. And courage and strength and hope and humor have to be bought and paid for with pain and work and prayers and tears.

JEROME P.
FLEISHMAN

Thirty-seven: *It's OK to Feel Guilty*

Complete these sentences:

If only...

_____

_____

_____

_____

I regret...

_____

_____

_____

I wish I had...

_____

_____

_____

I wish I hadn't...

_____

_____

_____

*To suffer one's death
and to be reborn
is not easy.*

FRITZ PERLS

Maybe if I had… ....
....
~~~~~~
~~~~~~
~~~~~~

Maybe if I hadn't… ....
~~~~~~
~~~~~~
~~~~~~
~~~~~~

I still feel guilty because… _____
~~~~~~
~~~~~~
~~~~~~
~~~~~~

I have guilt that… _____
~~~~~~
~~~~~~
~~~~~~
~~~~~~

*Run away
run and run
away
quickly
and do not
look back
ever
for I shall
consider that
encouragement
to follow run
run and run
quickly away
quickly.*

iamsorry!

Draw a picture of what your guilt looks and feels like.

A Healing Meditation
for Guilt and Resentment

Imagine a white light surrounding your body. Let it fill you with healing and grace. Know that only that which is for your highest good can take place during this meditation.

Imagine the white light focusing on the area of your body in which you experience guilt and resentment: your stomach, perhaps your heart, maybe your head (where are stored the beliefs about the way you and others *must, should* and *have to* behave.)

Let this light surround the guilt and resentment completely. Let it lift the guilt and resentment from your body.

Imagine your guilt and resentment, surrounded by this light, hovering in front of you. How big is it? What shape is it? What color is it? Is it making any sounds or noises? Does it have anything to say to you?

Now imagine the light penetrating the guilt and resentment. Let the light permeate the guilt and resentment. The more the light saturates the guilt and resentment, the lighter they become.

Imagine the guilt and resentment entirely diffused in the light. Like the darkness in a room when you turn on the light, the guilt and resentment are no more. There is nothing left but light.

Now, let this light return to the area(s) of your body where you experienced the guilt and resentment. Let this light make a new home in these areas. Imagine the light "cleaning up" any residual guilt and resentment in these areas.

Imagine that any new guilt or resentment, as it goes to "move into" that part of your body, is automatically surrounded, diffused and dissolved by that light, leaving only light.

Thank yourself for using your power to heal yourself.

Grief melts away
Like snow in May,
As if there were no
such cold thing.

GEORGE HERBERT
1633

Thirty-eight: *You May Want to Hire a Professional or Two*

Here is a partial list of those involved in the profession of healing.

- Alcohol and substance abuse counselors

- Chiropractors

- Clinical psychologists

- Exercise and fitness trainers

- Homeopaths

- Licensed hypnotherapists

- Marriage, child and family counselors

- Massage therapists

- Medical doctors and other health practitioners

- Nurse practitioners

- Nutritionists

- Pastoral counselors

- Psychiatrists

- Social workers

- Stress management counselors

In addition to whatever you're already doing, are you drawn to any of these professions to help speed your recovery, healing and growth? If so, make an appointment to see one (or more).

One out of four people in this country is mentally imbalanced. Think of your three closest friends— and if they seem okay, then you're the one.

ANN LANDERS

Thirty-nine: *When You Might Want Counseling or Therapy*

Do any of these statements apply to you?

> "I fear doing actual damage to someone else or myself—including acting on suicidal thoughts."

> "I seek solace in alcohol, drugs, overeating or other potentially harmful activities."

> "I find the support of wise friends and family is not enough."

> "I repeatedly find myself in loss situations."

> "I don't feel good about myself, and am perpetually out of control or under strain most of the time."

If any one of them applies, it might be time to shop for a therapist. This can be as much fun as any other shopping. Remember: it's OK to browse—you don't have to buy!

Ask understanding friends, coworkers, family members or your family doctor for recommendations. It's no shame to say, "I think I may need a little professional help with this loss. Can you recommend any good counselors or therapists?"

Have the courage to use *everything* available as tools for your surviving, healing and growth—and that may include a counselor or therapist.

Forty: *A Complete Medical Workup May Be in Order*

You might want to get a complete medical workup (physical exam, blood tests, the works). It's probably long overdue, anyway.

There are some illnesses triggered by loss, and there are some physical illnesses that *feel* like loss, even though the cause is physical.

Now might be a good time to take a look at the functioning of your body.

Your health-care provider can best advise you.

If there is anything you fear you *might* discover, remember that knowledge is better (and more powerful) than fear.

Call your doctor.

Make an appointment for a complete medical checkup.

Keep your appointment.

Never go to a doctor whose office plants have died.

ERMA BOMBECK

Forty-one: *Some Depressions May Require Medication*

If your symptoms of depression (pages 80-81) seem severe or continue longer than normal, an hour spent with a good psychiatrist discussing your situation and evaluating your next course of action—including the option of medication—can be invaluable.

If you wonder whether you need antidepressant medication, visit a competent psychiatrist for consultation.

*Go not for every grief
to the physician,
nor for every quarrel
to the lawyer,
nor for every thirst
to the pot.*

GEORGE HERBERT
1651

Forty-two: *Nutrition*

Go eat a carrot.

Everything you see I owe to spaghetti.

SOPHIA LOREN

What are some of the ways you could enhance your healing through nutrition?

_____

_____

_____

_____

_____

_____

_____

_____

_____

_____

_____

_____

_____

_____

_____

Fear less, hope more;
eat less, chew more;
whine less,
breathe more;
talk less, say more;
hate less, love more;
and all good things
are yours.

SWEDISH PROVERB

Forty-three: *Remember: You're Vulnerable*

List some ways you can take
better care of your body:

_____

_____

_____

_____

_____

_____

_____

_____

_____

_____

_____

_____

*It's hard
to be soft.*

Go take a walk.

*My grandmother
started walking five
miles a day
when she was sixty.
She's ninety-five now,
and we don't know
where the hell she is.*

ELLEN DEGENERIA

Forty-four: *Beware of the Rebound*

What thoughts, feelings, or reactions do you
have from the poem to the right?

_____

_____

_____

_____

_____

_____

_____

_____

_____

_____

_____

_____

It's always
you & you & you
but it's really
me.
I'll try again
and gain again
and die again
and push on into the
night.
To be reborn by a
look and a touch.
And to hope again that
this time it will last,
and to know
it will not be the last.

Write your own poem about "The Rebound":

_____

_____

_____

_____

_____

_____

_____

_____

_____

_____

_____

_____

*The world
is full of cactus,
but we don't have
to sit on it.*

WILL FOLEY

*Oh, don't worry
about Alan...Alan
will always land on
somebody's feet.*

DOROTHY PARKER
(on the day her divorce
from Alan Campbell
became final)

Forty-five: *Under-Indulge in Addictive Activities*

What is an area you *may* find addicting?
(Alcohol, drugs, food, sex, smoking, spending, gambling, working, exercise, romantic love)

....

....

....

....

....

....

....

....

....

....

....

*O! that I were as great
As is my grief,
or lesser than my name,
Or that I could forget
what I have been,
Or not remember what
I must be now.*

SHAKESPEARE

Talk about this potential with a caring friend.

One of the most successful programs is the Twelve Step Program pioneered by Alcoholics Anonymous. Although designed to overcome alcohol addiction, it works for all addictions. The twelve steps are

1) We admitted we were powerless over our addiction—that our lives had become unmanageable.

2) Came to believe that a Power greater than ourselves could restore us to sanity.

3) Made a decision to turn our will and our lives over to the care of this Higher Power, *as we understood Him, Her, or It.*

4) Made a searching and fearless moral inventory of ourselves.

5) Admitted to our Higher Power, to ourselves, and to another human being the exact nature of our wrongs.

6) Were entirely ready to have our Higher Power remove all these defects of character.

7) Humbly asked our Higher Power to remove our shortcomings.

8) Made a list of all persons we had harmed, and became willing to make amends to them all.

9) Made direct amends to such people wherever possible, except when to do so would injure them or others.

10) Continued to take personal inventory and when we were wrong, promptly admitted it.

11) Sought, through prayer and meditation, to improve our conscious contact with our Higher Power *as we understood Him, Her, or It,* praying only for knowledge of our Higher Power's will for us and the power to carry that out.

12) Having had a spiritual awakening as the result of these steps, we tried to carry this message to others and to practice these principles in all our affairs.

Would any (or all?) of these steps benefit you in your life?

I don't know what your destiny will be, but one thing I know: the only ones among you who will be really happy are those who will have sought and found how to serve.

ALBERT
SCHWEITZER

One of the primary addictions that haunt those in loss is negative thoughts.

What are the negative thoughts that plague you?

_____

_____

_____

_____

_____

_____

_____

_____

_____

_____

_____

Our best friends and our worst enemies are our thoughts.
A thought can do us more good than a doctor or a banker or a faithful friend.
It can also do us more harm than a brick.

DR. FRANK CRANE

Those negative thoughts are not true—or, if they are true, they're true only a small portion of the time. They're lies that lie in wait, and attack us when we're most vulnerable.

One of the best ways to counteract negative thoughts is being aware of them—knowing which *specific* negative thoughts we repeat to ourselves.

What are yours?

It's my fault, If I'd only...

I gave my best and it wasn't good enough.

Nothing I did was good enough.

When these appear in the future, simply say to yourself, "Oh, that's one of those negative thoughts. It's not true. I can go on and think about something else now."

Choose at least one thing on this list and do it *NOW*.

- Take a hot bath (no matter how you feel, thirty minutes after taking a hot bath you'll feel a lot better).

- Give or get a massage (rough and vigorous or slow and sensual).

- Snack on hot milk and cookies before bed.

- Buy yourself something you'd really enjoy.

- Treat yourself to your favorite double-dip ice-cream cone (with sprinkles).

- Get a manicure, pedicure or any other cure.

- Take a trip.

- Bask in the sun.

- Read a good book.

- Watch a good video.

- Take time for yourself.

- Buy yourself a cashmere anything.

- Go to a fine restaurant.

- See a good movie, play, opera, horse race.

- Visit an art museum.

- Buy yourself a bouquet of flowers.

- Acquiesce to your whims.

- Enjoy!

A little of what you fancy does you good.

MARIE LLOYD

We said…

NOW!

When you go to bed tonight, ask to remember a dream. Keep this page open and a pen nearby. When you awaken (in the morning or during the night), write or draw any thoughts, dreams or impressions you may have.

....

....

....

....

....

....

....

....

What message does the dream have for you?

....

....

....

....

....

When I lost my possessions I found my creativity. I felt I was being born for the first time.

YIP HARBURG

Forty-eight: *Sleep Patterns May Change*

Early morning awakening and midnight madness will soon pass.
In the meantime, here's a blank page to draw or doodle
until everything's back to normal.

This sleep difficulty shall pass.
If it persists or becomes too much of a problem, see your doctor.
If you're sleeping more than usual, put down the book and take a nap.

Forty-nine: *Sexual Desire May Change*

Have you had any change in your sexual desire or functioning? If so, write about it below.

_____

_____

_____

_____

_____

_____

_____

_____

_____

_____

_____

Now, preface each sentence above with, "It's OK that..."

There are as many nights as days, and the one is just as long as the other in the year's course. Even a happy life cannot be without a measure of darkness, and the word "happy" would lose its meaning if it were not balanced by sadness. It is far better to take things as they come along with patience and equanimity.

CARL JUNG

Fifty: *Remaining Distraught Is No Proof of Love*

Fill in the blanks:

Without *a lover,*
it's OK to enjoy *living.*
Without *a job,*
it's OK to enjoy *leisure time.*
Without *knowing if I'll be here tomorrow,*
it's OK to enjoy *today.*
Without _____
it's OK to enjoy _____
Without _____
it's OK to enjoy _____
Without _____
it's OK to enjoy _____
Without _____
it's OK to enjoy _____
Without _____
it's OK to enjoy _____
Without _____
it's OK to enjoy _____

*Expecting
heaven
is what
hell
is all
about.*

Sunlight is the source of all life and warmth on earth. Light is also the source of healing and growing. The use of the light through visualization has proven so effective that by many it is now considered a part of standard medical treatment.

Close your eyes (after reading this page).

Imagine yourself surrounded, filled and protected by goodness and light. Breathe deeply of this abundance. Feel the goodness and light dissolving any negativity or darkness in your mind, body and emotions.

Relax.

Enjoy.

Love is never lost. If not reciprocated, it will flow back and soften and purify the heart.

WASHINGTON
IRVING

Beliefs are personal, sacred things.
Write your own prayer, meditation
or contemplation below:

....

....

....

....

....

....

....

....

....

....

....

....

....

....

*Any action
performed before
an altar
can be considered
altering.*

Fifty-three: *Keep a Journal*

Write about anything in your life:

....

....

....

....

....

....

....

....

....

....

....

....

....

....

*Keep a diary and some-
day it'll keep you.*

MAE WEST

Did you enjoy that? Did you get value from that? Was it good for you? If so, you might want to buy a blank book (or computer disk) and keep a journal of your own.

Fifty-four: *There Is a Beauty in Sadness*

Write a poem about sadness:

_____

_____

_____

_____

_____

_____

_____

_____

_____

_____

_____

_____

Life has many secrets.

Where you are tonight is one of them.

Another: Why, really, did you go.

The world holds many wonders.

You are one of them.

Fifty-five: *Let Yourself Heal Fully*

Imagine yourself fully healed, fully functioning, fully grown.

What do you want your new life to include?

....

....

....

....

What do you want and need?

....

....

....

....

You deserve to heal fully. Desire it.

Nobody can walk into death and walk back out the same person. Everybody else, no matter who they are, whether they are a poet, a man of power, a frightened little child, whoever it is, they are afraid of the limitless possibilities of their own nature. Once you have nothing, you can be anything, and that's a feeling of freedom.

TED ROSENTHAL

Draw yourself fully healed...

Fifty-six: *Affirm Yourself*

Write, draw, say aloud, sing or dance each of the following affirmations.

- I am alive. I will survive.

- I am healing.

- I surrender to the process of healing.

- I am healing fully.

- I am healing naturally.

- I am gentle with myself.

- My broken heart is mending.

- I am stronger.

- I have the courage to grow.

- I am grateful for so much.

- My patience will outlast my pain.

When you tell yourself you're healing, what are the limiting voices that tell you "No you're not!"? Say aloud "I am healing" several times and write down what the limiting voice says:

I am healing	*No you're not.*
I am healing	*But I'm scared.*
I am healing	*It's getting worse.*
I am healing	*Nobody loves me.*
I am healing	
I am healing	
I am healing	
I am healing	
I am healing	
I am healing	
I am healing	
I am healing	
I am healing	
I am healing	
I am healing	
I am healing	
I am healing	
I am healing	

Strong people are made by opposition like kites that go up against the wind.

FRANK HARRIS

Fifty-seven: *Visualization*

Cut from magazines, newspapers, etc. pictures of where you will be soon, images of the life you want to live. Glue them on the facing page. (Use a larger sheet of paper if you like.) Hang your "positive collage" where you will see it often.

Visualize yourself as sound, healthy and filled with the vitality and boundless life of your Creator. Look upon yourself as the unique individual that you are. Get in harmony with the creative, life-giving, health-maintaining forces of the universe. Affirm peace, wholeness, and good health— and they will be yours.

NORMAN VINCENT
PEALE

Hang your positive collage
where you will see it often!

Get a package of construction paper.

Look at each sheet, each color, one at a time.

How does each color make you feel?

Make a pile of the colors that make you feel more cheerful, uplifted and "positive."

Review the "positive" pile.

How can you add
more of these colors to your life?
(HINTS: Clothing, food, fabrics, pictures, lighting.)

....

....

....

....

....

....

....

*Death is not putting
out the light.
It is extinguishing the
candle because the
dawn has come!*

SALESIAN
MISSIONS

Fifty-nine: *Laugh!*

- Call at least three people you know and ask them to tell you a joke or humorous story. (If they have a poor sense of humor, it might even be funnier.)

- Rent a funny video and watch it.

- Get a funny book and read it.

- Buy a comedy album and listen to it.

- Watch a TV sitcom.

What's the second funniest thing that ever happened to you?

_____

_____

_____

_____

_____

_____

Humor is an affirmation of dignity, a declaration of man's superiority to all that befalls him.

ROMAN GARY

I am a marvelous housekeeper. Every time I leave a man I keep his house.

ZSA ZSA GABOR

What's the funniest thing
that ever happened to you?

....

....

....

....

....

....

He who laughs, lasts.

MARY PETTIBONE
POOLE

What's the funniest thing
that happened to you today?
("A funny thing happened on the way to decorum…")

....

....

....

....

....

....

*Being divorced
is like being hit by a
Mack truck.
If you live through it,
you start looking
very carefully to the
right and to the left.*

JEAN KERR

131

Sixty: *As Healing Continues...*

What progress have you made?

....

....

....

*If you would not have
affliction
visit you twice,
listen at once
to what it teaches.*

JAMES BURGH

What has healed?

....

....

....

How has your thinking sharpened?

....

....

....

How has your judgement
become sounder and more reliable ?

....

....

....

How have your concentration and memory improved?

....

....

....

How have you had a desire to be more with others?

....

....

....

How have you had a desire to do more for others?

....

....

....

What progress have you made?

....

....

....

You're well on your way! Appreciate your efforts.

*Suffering
is a revelation.
One discovers things
one never
discovered before.*

OSCAR WILDE

GROWING

*Experience is not
what happens to a man.
It is what a man does with
what happens to him.*

ALDOUS HUXLEY

Sixty-one: *You're Stronger Now*

What have you learned about loss
and about yourself?

I can survive.

The pain eventually lessens.

Healing does occur.

Draw a picture of what your inner strength looks and feels like.

Sixty-two: *Let Go of the Loss and Move On*

Imagine yourself attached to your loss with a rope. The rope has a knot in it. Imagine yourself untying this knot, saying good-bye to your loss, releasing the rope, turning from the loss, and moving on.

How do you feel?

_____

_____

_____

Is anything tugging at you or holding you back? If so, what?

_____

_____

_____

Imagine cutting those ties. What feelings do you have about leaving the loss behind?

_____

_____

_____

*We have come
over a way that
with tears
has been watered.*

JAMES WELDON
JOHNSON

Can you tolerate the joy of moving on?

....

....

....

What specific next step do you need to take
in your life to move on?

....

....

....

....

Are you willing to take it?

....

....

....

*There are tears of grief
and tears of joy, but
I've yet
to see someone
whose eyes have
grown red
from tears of joy.*

MORITZ SAPHIR

Now?

SO,

TAKE IT!

(Take it easy, but take it.)

Sixty-three: *Forgiveness is Letting Go*

Forgiveness lightens the heaviness of loss. It allows you to set down your burdens and never pick them up again.

Imagine a burden you still have regarding the loss. (For example, a feeling of betrayal, resentment, hurt, mistreatment or jealousy.)

See yourself setting this burden down, onto a beam of white light. The light lightens and dissolves the burden. As the burden dissolves, say to it, "I release you into the light, and I am free." The burden dissolves completely.

What other burden are you carrying? (Perhaps fear, anger, envy, exhaustion.) Place that into the beam of light. As it dissolves, say, "I release you into the light, and I am free."

Repeat this process with any other burdens that surface.

Forgiveness is the key to action and freedom.

HANNAH ARENDT

The reason to forgive is not so much for the other person but for you— your peace of mind and the quality of all your future love relationships.

HAROLD H.
BLOOMFIELD

Sixty-four: *Forgive the Other Person*

Imagine the person you lost (or the person primarily responsible for your loss) standing in the beam of light. Say to him or her, "I forgive you." Each time you say "I forgive you," record the emotional reaction within yourself.

"I forgive you"	*No I don't.*
"I forgive you"	*I hate you.*
"I forgive you"	*OK, so go.*
"I forgive you"	
"I forgive you"	
"I forgive you"	
"I forgive you"	
"I forgive you"	
"I forgive you"	
"I forgive you"	
"I forgive you"	
"I forgive you"	
"I forgive you"	
"I forgive you"	
"I forgive you"	

Without forgiveness life is governed by an endless cycle of resentment and retaliation.

ROBERTO ASSAGLIOLI

When you're finished, say, "I release you into the light, and I walk free."

Sixty-five: *Forgive Yourself*

Imagine yourself in the column of light. See and feel yourself as clearly as possible. Say to yourself, "I forgive myself." Each time you say it, record below your emotional reactions.

"I forgive myself"   *Who am I to forgive myself?*

"I forgive myself"   *Ha!*

"I forgive myself"   *Well, maybe.*

"I forgive myself"

"I forgive myself"

"I forgive myself"

"I forgive myself"

"I forgive myself"

"I forgive myself"

"I forgive myself"

"I forgive myself"

"I forgive myself"

"I forgive myself"

"I forgive myself"

"I forgive myself"

"I forgive myself"

Say to yourself, "I release all my burdens into the light, and I am free." See yourself joyful, happy and free, stepping into your future with peace, love and grace.

Sixty-six: *Take Stock of the Good*

In what ways is your life better, deeper and richer thanks to your relationship with the thing or person you lost?
(EXAMPLES: I learned how to ski; I moved; I met new people.)

_____

_____

_____

_____

_____

_____

_____

_____

_____

_____

*Love
is the most
written about
talked about
laughed about
and
cried about*

human emotion.

*I once said:
"I will never
write about
love."*

And then

I loved.

Sixty-seven: *You Are a Better Person for Having Loved*

What are the qualities of your heart
enhanced by the fact that you have loved?

Wisdom,   *Caring,*

Compassion, Flexibility,   *Forgiveness, Resiliency,*

Trust, Spirit, Courage, Tolerance,   *Warmth, Acceptance, Experience*

Draw a picture of the "better" you,
or write a poem about your growth.

Sixty-eight: *Praise Yourself for the Courage to Relate*

Successfully surviving a loss has its lessons,
some fortunate, some not-so-fortunate.

Limiting Lesson	Expansive Lesson
I need to keep others at arm's length.	Arms are for reaching out and opening to others.
Intimacy is painful.	I enjoy closeness.
I am not loveable.	I am worthy of love just as I am.
Relationships are too costly.	I can't afford not to love.
I don't trust my choices in love.	I can make new and better choices.
I always wind up getting hurt.	I create my own relationships and my reactions to them.
I am surrounded by fear and rejection.	I am surrounded by loving.
People will cheat me if they can.	I can create safe, trusting relationships.

On the left, list the limiting lesson of loss you have learned.
On the right, list its expansive counterpart.
Feel free to "steal" from our list on the facing page.

Limiting Lesson   Expansive Lesson

Sixty-nine: *Changes*

Write each of these sentences five times. If any limitations, doubts or fears arise as you write these, say to yourself out loud, "This affirmation is true."

I, _____, am ready for my next exciting adventure.

I, _____

I, _____

I, _____

I, _____

I, _____

I, _____, am a fun-loving, affectionate person.

I, _____

I, _____

I, _____

I, _____

I, _____

I, _____, have all I need in order to succeed.

I, _____

I, _____

I, _____

I, _____

I, _____

This cup holds grief and balm in equal measure. Light, darkness. Who drinks from it must change.

MAY SARTON

I, _____, deserve to be loved and accepted just as I am.

I, _____

I, _____

I, _____

I, _____

I, _____

I, _____, appreciate and love myself and others.

I, _____

I, _____

I, _____

I, _____

I, _____

I, _____, am beautiful.

I, _____

I, _____

I, _____

I, _____

I, _____

*Change
is the handmaiden
Nature requires
to do
her miracles with.*

MARK TWAIN

Write your own affirmations here:

*What we see
depends mainly
on what we look for.*

JOHN LUBBOCK

Pick any affirmation and write it here 20 times:

_I keep the telephone
of my mind
open to peace,
harmony, health, love
and abundance.
Then,
whenever doubt,
anxiety or fear
try to call me,
they keep getting a
busy signal—
and they'll soon
forget my number._

EDITH ARMSTRONG

You've already started setting new goals and areas to explore. Make a list of those. When done, tear out this page and put it someplace you can have access to it. Add to the list as you think of other goals.

Every man has to seek in his own way to make his own self more noble and to realize his own true worth.

ALBERT
SCHWEITZER

_____

_____

_____

_____

_____

_____

_____

_____

_____

_____

Say aloud "I want..." about each goal.
How does that feel?

A helpful book to guide you in achieving your goals is called *DO IT! Let's Get Off Our Buts,* available in bookstores or by calling 1-800-LIFE-101.

Seventy-one: *Invite New People into Your Life*

- Have cards printed with your name and phone number.

- Call someone you'd like to know better and arrange a time to get together.

- Go alone to a concert, play, meeting or any public gathering. Plan to meet someone new.

- Treat old friends as if they were new.

- Treat a stranger as if he or she were an old friend.

- Do a task that needs doing (shopping, getting the car washed) and leave enough time in the process to meet others.

- Meet a neighbor.

- Carry a pen and paper for exchanging phone numbers.

"I feel an affinity for you..."

I guess that's as close as clever people ever come to saying "I love you"

On the first date.

When meeting others, use "How?" "Why?" and "Tell me more." If you say nothing more than these three things in an hour of conversation, you will be seen by others as a brilliant conversationalist.

Seventy-two: *Develop New Interests*

Make a list of the things you are curious about, or find even remotely interesting:

_____

_____

_____

_____

_____

_____

_____

_____

_____

_____

*There
you were,
dancing.*

*I saw only
your back first.
Then a hint
of your profile.
But even then I knew
my search had found
in you a fulfillment.*

The long search.

*The search
I would abandon,
and then realize
the search
included that
abandonment.*

*There
you were,
dancing.*

Pick one. Take at least one action step toward pursuing it (make a phone call, buy a book, call someone who knows something about it).

Seventy-three: But Don't Forget the Old Interests

Make a list of activities you find fascinating and fulfilling—especially the ones you may not have pursued during your period of recovery:

_____

_____

_____

_____

_____

_____

_____

_____

_____

*You never really know
a man
until you have
divorced him.*

ZSA ZSA GABOR

Guess what we're going to ask you to do?

Look in the Yellow Pages under "Clubs," "Associations," "Athletic Organizations," "Fraternal Organizations," "Youth Organizations," and read the listings. Make a note here of any that sound interesting. Call at least three and ask for further information. Attend at least one meeting.

Your imperfections only draw me closer to you.

they remind me that you're human.

that with humans I have a chance.

Do one or more of the following:

- Call at least three people and let them know three things you appreciate about them.

- Put on your favorite uplifting song and dance. (ADVANCED VERSION: Sing while you dance.)

- Make a list of ten things you enjoy:

I enjoy _____

I enjoy _____

I enjoy _____

I enjoy _____

I enjoy _____

I enjoy _____

I enjoy _____

I enjoy _____

I enjoy _____

I enjoy _____

Deep down
I'm pretty superficial.

AVA GARDNER

- Practice saying, "I would prefer it if you..." as a way of communicating your wants and desires. Tell someone what you would prefer.

Make a list of ten things you care about:

I care about _____

I care about _____

I care about _____

I care about _____

I care about _____

I care about _____

I care about _____

I care about _____

I care about _____

I care about _____

Mental Health Rules
1. HAVE A HOBBY: Acquire pursuits which absorb your interest; sports and "nature" are best.
2. DEVELOP A PHILOSOPHY: Adapt yourself to social and spiritual surroundings.
3. SHARE YOUR THOUGHTS: Cultivate companionship in thought and in feeling. Confide, confess, consult.
4. FACE YOUR FEARS: Analyze them; daylight dismisses ghosts.
5. BALANCE FANTASY WITH FACT: Dream but also do; wish but build; imagine but ever face reality.
6. BEWARE ALLURING ESCAPES: Alcohol, opiates and barbitals may prove faithless friends.
7. EXERCISE: Walk, swim, golf—muscles need activity.
8. LOVE, BUT LOVE WISELY: Sex is a flame which uncontrolled may scorch; properly guided, it will light the torch of eternity.
9. DON'T BECOME ENGULFED IN A WHIRLPOOL OF WORRIES: Call early for help. The doctor is ready for your rescue.
10. TRUST IN TIME: Be patient and hopeful, time is a great therapist.

DR. JOSEPH
FETTERMAN

Make a list of ten things you no longer want to do:

_____

_____

_____

_____

_____

_____

_____

_____

_____

_____

*I'm as pure
as the driven slush.*

TALLULAH
BANKHEAD

*Don't think it hasn't
been charming,
because it hasn't.*

MARGOT ASQUITH

Seventy-six: *Your Words Have Power*

What are some of your "shoulds"?

I should always be nice. I should exercise.

What are your "nevers"?

You never do what I say. I never hurt other people.

What do you "hope" for?

I hope I'll be happy. I hope they will call.

Cast of Characters

I Won't is a tramp,
I Can't is a quitter,
I Don't Know is lazy,
I Wish I Could
is a wisher,
I Might is waking up,
I Will Try is on his feet,
I Can is on his way,
I Will is at work,
I Did is now the boss.

EARL CASSEL

What do you "try" to do?

I'm trying to lose weight. I'm trying to give up smoking.

What do you "wish" for?

I wish I had a new car. I wish I felt better.

What are your "maybes"?

Maybe I'll visit Italy. Maybe I'll do this exercise.

Some questions don't have answers, which is a terribly difficult lesson to learn.

KATHERINE GRAHAM

What are your "musts"?

I must always be successful. You must not be angry with me.

—————————————————————

—————————————————————

—————————————————————

—————————————————————

Now that I'm over sixty I'm veering toward respectability.

SHELLEY WINTERS

You must now rewrite—oops!—we would *prefer* it if you would now rewrite each of your sentences.

- Replace "should" and "must" with "prefer"

- Replace "never" with "seldom"

- Replace "I hope," "I'm trying," "I wish," and "Maybe" with "I will" or "I plan."

Turn all of your "should" statements on page 162 into "I prefer" statements.

I prefer to always be nice. I prefer to exercise.

—————————————————————

—————————————————————

—————————————————————

—————————————————————

Turn your "never" statements on page 162 into "seldom" statements.

You seldom do what I say. I seldom hurt other people.

_____

_____

_____

_____

Search for the seed of good in every adversity. Master that principle and you will own a precious shield that will guard you well through all the darkest valleys you must traverse. Stars may be seen from the bottom of a deep well, when they cannot be discerned from the mountaintop. So will you learn things in adversity that you would never have discovered without trouble. There is always a seed of good. Find it and prosper.

OG MANDINO

Turn your "hope" statements on page 162 into statements of what you "plan" to do.

I plan to be happy. I'm planning that they will call.

_____

_____

_____

_____

Turn your "try" statements on page 163
into "do" statements.

I'm losing weight. I'm giving up smoking.

_____

_____

_____

Turn your "wish" statements on page 163
into statements of what you are going to
"move" on.

I'm moving on getting a new car. I'm moving in the direc-

tion of feeling better.

_____

_____

_____

Turn your "maybe" statements on page 163
into planned "action" statements.

I'll visit Italy. I'll do this exercise.

Turn your "must" statements on page 164
into statements of what you "prefer."

I would prefer to always be successful. I would prefer if you

were not angry with me.

Seventy-seven: *Think "Both/And" Rather Than "Either/Or"*

What are your either/or beliefs?

I'm either good or bad.

I'm either a success or a failure.

Relationships (cars, people, TV shows, etc.) are either good or bad.

They either like me or dislike me.

The sense of humor is the oil of life's engine. Without it, the machinery creaks and groans. No lot is so hard, no aspect of things is so grim, but it relaxes before a hearty laugh.

G. S. MERRIAM

Change "either" to "both" and "or" to "and" in each sentence.

I'm both good and bad.

I'm both a success and a failure.

Relationships (cars, people, TV shows, etc.) are both good and bad.

They both like me and dislike me.

*She's my best friend.
I hate her.*

RICHMAL
CROMPTON

Seventy-eight: *The Freedom to Choose*

I choose _____

The steps I'm taking to obtain that choice are

_____

_____

_____

I choose _____

The steps I'm taking to obtain that choice are

_____

_____

_____

I choose _____

The steps I'm taking to obtain that choice are

_____

_____

_____

I choose _____

The steps I'm taking to obtain that choice are

_____

_____

_____

I choose _____

The steps I'm taking to obtain that choice are

_____

_____

_____

*One ought
every day at least
to hear a little song,
read a good poem,
see a fine picture, and,
if it were possible,
to speak a few
reasonable words.*

GOETHE

Seventy-nine: *It's OK to Ask*

Think about ways other people can help you
obtain the goals you have chosen.
Make a list of these people and what they can do to help:

Person   Help Requested

Betty   *Help me paint my apartment*

Eighty: *It's OK for Others to Say No*

Go through the previous list and list a specific alternate action that will get you closer to the goal if each person says no:

Paint my own apartment (or hire painters) if Betty won't help me.

Your kindness is cruel.

*People afraid
of inflicting
pain are awfully painful
to be around.*

*A rejection
somewhere near
the beginning
would have been
easy to take,
but your*

*no now.
ow.*

Eighty-one: *It's OK for Others to Say Yes*

If each person on the previous list says yes, which of your limiting beliefs about yourself will be challenged? Write what's true. Enjoy the vision of other people's support.

I don't deserve their help./I do deserve their help.

I would like you to like me

but

I would love you to love me.

Eighty-two: *Fear Can Be a Friend*

What are your fears?

How can you convert your fear into excitement and adventure?

Fear	Affirmation
I'll be rejected.	*I can handle whatever happens, and I may be accepted.*
I'll be accepted.	*I can handle whatever happens, and I enjoy being accepted.*
They won't love me.	*I'll love myself, and they may love me.*

Prepare to meet an old friend: *excitement*—better known, perhaps, as fear. On the next page (don't turn the page!) are six activities, any one of which is designed to create excitement in the average human being.

Circle a number below:

1   2   3   4   5   6

Now, do the activity on the next page that corresponds to the number you chose.

1. Draw the shades, get completely naked, put on your least favorite radio station, and dance around your living room.

2. Call three friends and ask to be fixed up on a blind date. (If you're married—or not yet ready for dating—ask your friends to introduce you to someone new whom you might also enjoy as a friend.)

3. Attend an entertainment form you would not normally attend (opera, mud wrestling, roller derby).

4. Go to an ethnic restaurant and order a dish you would otherwise not choose.

5. Buy an item of clothing you normally would not buy and wear it all day (cowboy hat, flamboyant scarf, stretch pants, shorts, tie-dyed T-shirt).

6. Call someone who feels "wronged" by you and apologize—whether you feel responsible or not.

If you want to conquer fear, don't sit at home and think about it. Go out and get busy.

DALE CARNEGIE

What was living that adventure like? What did you learn?

_____

_____

_____

_____

_____

_____

_____

_____

_____

_____

_____

_____

_____

_____

I am terribly shy,
but of course no one
believes me.
Come to think of it,
neither would I.

CAROL CHANNING

Eighty-three: *The Antidote for Anxiety Is Action*

What is it in your life that you know needs doing, but you are afraid to do?

....

....

....

....

....

....

What is the next action step you can take for each fear?

....

....

....

....

....

....

What seems clear,
is that laughter
is an antidote
to apprehension
and panic.
As such,
its value is not less
than that of
the fire extinguisher
that puts out the flame.

NORMAN COUSINS

Do the next action step for at least three of the fears on the previous page.

What were your experiences and results?

_____

_____

_____

_____

_____

_____

_____

_____

_____

_____

*There is a land
of the living and a
land of the dead,
and the bridge is love.*

THORNTON WILDER

179

Eighty-four: *Postpone Procrastination*

Practice your procrastination by putting off doing each of the following:

Read every book you ever purchased but have not yet read.

List three ways or good reasons for not doing this:

_____

_____

_____

Do all the exercise you said you would do during the past year.

List three ways or good reasons for not doing this:

_____

_____

_____

Visit every member of your family for at least a week no matter where they live and never lose your temper or your patience.

List three ways or good reasons for not doing this:

....

....

....

(Harold, please write four more for this list.)—Melba

(Melba, any more suggestions?)—Peter

(Peter, you're so good at coming up with these, why don't you finish these?)—Harold

Books come at my call and return when I desire them; they are never out of humor and they answer all my questions with readiness. Some present in review before me the events of past ages; others reveal to me the secrets of Nature. These teach me how to live, and those how to die; these dispel my melancholy by their mirth, and amuse me by their sallies of wit. Some there are who prepare my soul to suffer everything, to desire nothing, and to become thoroughly acquainted with itself.

PETRARCH

When you are reminded of your loss, it's a good idea to have something else to think about or do—the more specific the better. Why not plan ahead?

List ten positive, life-enhancing things you will do (or think about) the next time you are reminded of your loss:

....

....

....

....

....

....

....

....

....

....

The next time you are reminded of your loss, turn to this page and do (or think about) one of these things.

Four ducks on a pond,
A grass bank beyond,
A blue sky of spring,
White clouds
on the wing;
What a little thing
To remember
for years—
To remember
with tears!

WILLIAM
ALLINGHAM

What are the next three significant dates connected to your loss (the date you met, the date of the loss, significant birthday, major holidays, etc.)? Write them here:

1. _____

_____

2. _____

_____

3. _____

_____

What comforting, nurturing, uplifting activities can you plan now to do on those dates?

1. _____

_____

2. _____

_____

3. _____

_____

Plan them.

Grief can take care of itself, but to get the full value of a joy you must have somebody to divide it with.

MARK TWAIN

Eighty-seven: *Solitude*

Spend the next hour alone, doing something that allows you to interact with yourself.

Suggestions:

- Take a walk.
- Write a poem.
- Take a hot bath.
- Meditate.
- Lie in bed doing nothing.
- Draw a picture.
- Build a fire and sit by it.
- Look (really *look*) at a flower.

Silence is healing for all ailments.

HEBREW PROVERB

Spend the next hour
doing something creative.

Suggestions:

- Draw, paint or doodle something.

- Write a journal entry, letter, poem, chapter or scene.

- Cook something you've never made before.

- Sew (not just mending—something creative).

- Make up a new word for something that doesn't have a word. (Like the feeling you get when you gently rub the tip of your tongue along the roof of your mouth.)

- Sculpt, mold or shape something.

- Write a song.

- Sing a song.

- Play something—on an instrument, gameboard, field or court.

- Make up an alternate list to this one.

When I create something it doesn't hurt as much.

Maybe that's why God created me.

Eighty-nine: *Enjoy!*

Make a list of ten things you enjoy doing:

....

....

....

....

....

....

....

....

Do one of them *now*.

*We know too much
and feel too little.*

BERTRAND RUSSELL

Ninety: *Appreciation*

Look around where you are *right now* and find something to appreciate. Look especially for those often overlooked or taken-for-granted things (colors, the design of a chair, light reflected through a bottle of water).

Take a while to appreciate it, write it down, and find something else. Do this *at least* ten times—but, once you get into the habit, why not do it *all* the time?

There is no natural object unimportant or trifling. From the least of Nature's works he may learn the greatest lessons.

SIR JOHN HERSCHEL

Ninety-one: *Do Something for Someone Else*

Guess what we're going to ask you to do? Yes, you guessed it: Go do something for someone else.

This does not need to be a full-fledged Service Project. A quick review of your friends and associates will probably reveal someone who could use a helping hand at something.

Or, you can go out with the intention of being of service and see what comes to you. It could be as simple as giving directions to a lost tourist or buying a homeless person a Big Mac. When the person you're to do something for appears, you'll know.

One of the most amazing things ever said on this earth is Jesus' statement: "He that is greatest among you shall be your servant." Nobody has one chance in a billion of being thought really great after a century has passed except those who have been the servants of all. That strange realist from Bethlehem knew that.

HARRY EMERSON FOSDICK

We cannot hold a torch to light another's path without brightening our own.

BEN SWEETLAND

Ninety-two: *Appreciate Your Growth*

How have you grown? In what areas are you stronger, wiser, more capable and mature? Now's not the time for false modesty. You *have* grown. Admit it, claim it for yourself, and write it down:

_____

_____

_____

_____

_____

_____

_____

_____

_____

_____

*Getters generally
don't get happiness;
givers get it.
You simply give
to others
a bit of yourself—
a thoughtful act,
a helpful idea,
a word of appreciation,
a lift over
a rough spot,
a sense
of understanding,
a timely suggestion.
You take something
out of your mind,
garnished in kindness
out of your heart,
and put it into
the other fellow's
mind and heart.*

CHARLES H. BURR

Ninety-three: *Your Happiness Is Up to You*

Do you choose happiness now?

☐ Yes

☐ No

List the people who most helped you survive your loss:

_____

_____

_____

_____

_____

_____

_____

_____

_____

What would be the best way of thanking, acknowledging and celebrating your survival with these people? Notes? Gifts? A party? Whatever it would be, plan it now.

*Learn to wish
that everything
should come to pass
exactly as it does.*

EPICTETUS

CONGRATULATIONS!

Look in the mirror. Thank and congratulate the person who—more than anyone else— was responsible for your surviving, healing and growth: You.

Hello. This is Peter. I thought I'd tell you about some of the books published by Prelude Press. This may seem like a shameless commercial. It is not. As author (or co-author) and publisher of these books, I say it's not a commercial—it is an exercise in blatant egoism.

How to Survive the Loss of a Love

This is the new edition, completely revised and updated. 212 pages. **Hardcover**, $10.00. **Audio Tapes** (complete and unabridged, read by the authors, two cassettes), $9.99.

LIFE 101:
Everything We Wish We Had Learned
About Life in School—But Didn't

The overview book of the *LIFE 101 Series*. The idea behind *LIFE 101* is that everything in life is for our upliftment, learning and growth—including (and, perhaps, especially) the "bad" stuff. "The title jolly well says it all," said the *Los Angeles Times*—jolly well saying it all. 400 pages. **Paperback**, $5.99. **Hardcover**, $18.95. **Audio Tapes** (complete and unabridged, five cassettes), $19.99. **Wristwatch** (Paul LeBus designed), $35.00.

DO IT!
Let's Get Off Our Buts

DO IT! is a book for those who want to discover—clearly and precisely—their dream; who choose to pursue that dream even if it means learning (and—gasp!—practicing) new behavior; who wouldn't mind having some fun along the way; and who are willing to expand their comfort zone enough to include their heart's desire—and maybe even a dance floor. 496 pages. **Hardcover**, $20.00. **Audio Tapes** (complete and unabridged, six cassettes), $22.99.

You Can't Afford the Luxury of a Negative Thought

This is the first book John-Roger and I co-authored. In its 622 pages, we've done all that we can to make a "serious" subject (life-threatening illness) light. As we point out in the introduction, "This is not just a book for people with life-threatening illnesses. It's a book for anyone afflicted with one of the primary diseases of our time—negative thinking." **Trade paperback**, $15.00. **Audio Tapes** (complete and unabridged, eight cassettes), $22.99. **Wristwatch**, $35.00.

Focus on the Positive:
The *You Can't Afford the Luxury of a Negative Thought* Workbook

Specific exercises to help you eliminate the negative and latch onto the affirmative. **Trade paperback**, $12.00.

John-Roger's Meditation for Loving Yourself

This is the most beautiful meditation tape I know. It lasts a little over half an hour. The meditation is repeated on side two. (That way, all you have to do is turn the tape over—no rewinding.) John-Roger is "backed" by a lovely musical score composed and performed by Scott Fitzgerald and Rob Whitesides-Woo. The tape is $10 and highly recommended. This meditation is also included in the audio cassette package of *You Can't Afford the Luxury of a Negative Thought*. (It's on side two of tape eight. That means rewinding!)

I Marry You Because...

Poetry (by yours truly) and quotations (by truly good writers) on love and marriage. **Hardcover,** 87 pages, $11.95.

Come Love With Me & Be My Life:
The Collected Romantic Poetry of Peter McWilliams

Yes, it's been 25 years since my first book of poetry was published, and here's the 25-year anthology. 250 pages. **Hardcover,** $12.95. **Audio Tape** (complete and unabridged, read by guess who?), $12.95.

The Personal Computer Book

A compilation and updating of all my earlier introductory computer books. If you're looking for an enjoyable, nonintimidating introduction to what personal computers are and what they do, you'll enjoy this book. 672 pages. **Trade paperback,** $19.95.

Self-Publishing, Self-Taught

Everything I know about self-publishing, for those who want to know (unpublished writers, for example, who can't find a publisher, or published writers who want to lose their publisher). It costs a lot because we don't sell that many. (Maybe we don't sell that many because it costs a lot. Hmmmm.) $95.00.

To order any of these books, please check your local bookstore, or call

1-800-LIFE-101

or write to
Prelude Press
8165 Mannix Drive
Los Angeles, California 90046

Please, call or write for our free catalog!

About the Authors

MELBA COLGROVE, Ph.D., earned degrees in literature, foreign trade, special education, counseling and organizational psychology. She received her Ph.D. in 1966 from the University of Michigan, having written her doctoral dissertation on creative problem solving. Presently, she is writing and consulting from her home in Oxford, Michigan. She is also on the staff of Waterford Family Counseling in Waterford, Michigan.

HAROLD H. BLOOMFIELD, M.D., is one of the leading psychological educators of our time. An eminent Yale-trained psychiatrist, Dr. Bloomfield introduced meditation, holistic health and family peacemaking to millions of people. He is an Adjunct Professor of Psychology at Union Graduate School. A book he co-authored, *TM*, was on the *New York Times* bestseller list for over six months. Dr. Bloomfield is the co-author of other major bestsellers such as *How to Survive the Loss of a Love, Making Peace with Your Parents, Making Peace with Yourself, Inner Joy* and *Lifemates*. His books have sold over 5,000,000 copies and have been translated into twenty-two languages. Dr. Bloomfield is among the most sought-after keynote speakers and seminar leaders in the world for public audiences, educational programs and conferences. He is a frequent guest on the *Oprah Winfrey Show, Donahue, Sally Jesse Raphael* and CNN. His articles appear in such magazines as *Cosmopolitan, Ladies Home Journal, Health* and *New Woman.* Dr. Bloomfield is in the private practice of psychiatry and psychotherapy in Del Mar, California.

PETER McWILLIAMS published his first book, a collection of poetry, at the age of seventeen. His series of poetry books went on to sell more than 3,500,000 copies. A volume of his poetry and advice, *Surviving the Loss of a Love,* was the inspiration for this book. A book he co-authored on meditation was #1 on the *New York Times* bestseller list. His *The Personal Computer Book* was a bestseller. His *LIFE 101 Series* of books written with John-Roger were all bestsellers. (*DO IT!* was #1 on the *New York Times* hardcover list.) He is a nationally syndicated columnist, teaches seminars, and has appeared on the *Oprah Winfrey Show, Donahue, Larry King* and *The Today Show.*